HOW TO BE...

an ACTOR

Stephanie Turnbull

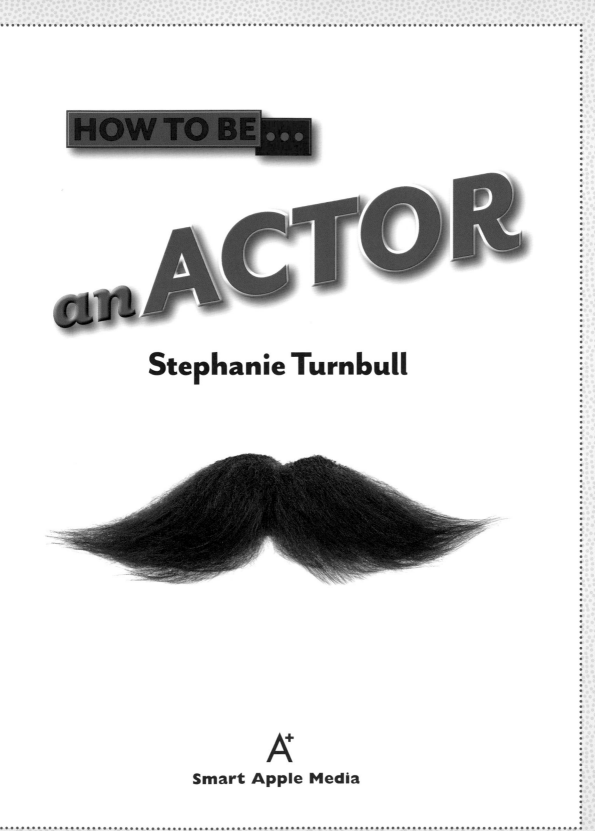

A⁺

Smart Apple Media

Published by Smart Apple Media, an imprint of Black Rabbit Books
P.O. Box 3263, Mankato, Minnesota, 56002
www.blackrabbitbooks.com

Printed in the United States of America, at Corporate Graphics
in North Mankato, Minnesota

Designed and illustrated by Guy Callaby
Edited by Mary-Jane Wilkins

Cataloging-in-Publication Data is available from the Library of Congress

ISBN 978-1-62588-364-3

Photo acknowledgements
t = top, b = bottom, c = centre, l = left, r = right
page 1 Mediagram; 3t Tracy Whiteside, l swissmacky, r KellyBoreson,
b prudkov/all Shutterstock; 4 Michelle Milliman/Thinkstock; 5 MANDY
GODBEHEAR/Shutterstock; 6 Fuse/Thinkstock; 8t Igor Bulgarin,
b savageultralight; 9 Elzbieta Sekowska; 11t DeSerg, c Alliance, b zkruger;
12t luckyraccoon/all Shutterstock, b Jupiterimages/Thinkstock;
13t Vibrant Image Studio, l LifePhotoStudio, r David Davis; 14 ESTUDI M6,
b Pressmaster; 16 Raisa Kanareva; 18t Igor Bulgarin/all Shutterstock,
c Loke Yek Mang/all Shutterstock, b George Bailey/Thinkstock; 19tl Egyptian
Studio, tr Luis Carlos Torres, c Madlen, r Piyato, b LeonP, 20 StepStock;
22 bikeriderlondon; 23 Pablo Hidalgo/all Shutterstock
Cover Pavel L Photo and Video/Shutterstock

DAD0060
022015
9 8 7 6 5 4 3 2 1

Contents

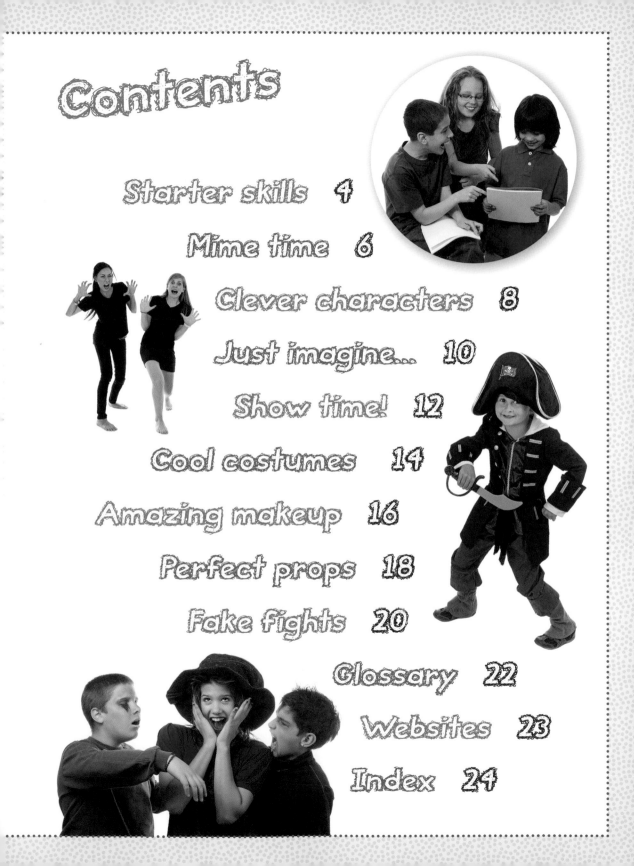

Starter skills

If you love to perform, dress up, and entertain your friends, try the brilliant acting tips and techniques in this book. One day you could be a great actor or a famous movie star!

Warm-up exercises

Do a few warm-up exercises first to prepare your body and brain for acting. It's more fun in a group!

1 Loosen up

Stretch and shake. Jog on the spot, dance, or play a quick game of tag. Stand in pairs and copy each other's movements as if you're looking in a mirror.

This helps you relax, concentrate, and work with other people.

2 Use your voice

Read out tongue twisters, a poem, or a page from a book. Choose a simple word such as "yes" or "no" and try saying it in as many different ways as you can.

This helps you speak clearly, loudly, and confidently.

Yes?

YEEESS!!!

3 Breathe deeply

Haaa...

Stand up straight with one hand on your stomach and take a slow, deep breath. Feel your stomach expand. Breathe out slowly with a gentle "haaa" sound until all the air is gone. Do this a few times.

This helps you stay calm and make sounds without straining your voice.

HANDY HINTS

Look out for the thumbs up. Here you'll find tips to help you build and improve your skills.

This warning hand is for important advice and safety facts.

Mime time

Miming means using expressions and movements to tell stories and show feelings. It's an important acting skill, so try these fun mime games with friends.

Yum or yuck?

1 Sit opposite a friend at a table and each imagine a plate of food in front of you. Think hard about what it is and how it smells. Is it delicious, disgusting, or unusual?

2 Now take turns to mime taking a mouthful. Guess what each other's food might be!

Mime moves

Here are two simple ways of practicing whole body mimes.

1 *Mime a simple action, such as climbing a ladder or opening a stiff door. Try to make your moves realistic.*

2 *Take turns to cross the room pretending to carry something—a tray of drinks, a bag of books, a wriggling puppy. Pass the invisible object to a friend and ask them what it is.*

 Give each other suggestions for items to carry.

WHAT NEXT? *Tell a fairy story through mime and see if a friend can guess which one it is!*

Clever characters

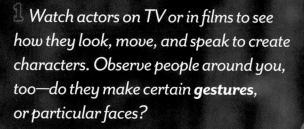

Acting means pretending to be someone else—and making that person seem real. Here are some top tips for getting into character.

1 Watch actors on TV or in films to see how they look, move, and speak to create characters. Observe people around you, too—do they make certain **gestures**, or particular faces?

Never try too hard to show emotions. It looks unrealistic!

2 *Invent a character. Write down their name, age, and family history. Are they old or young? Healthy or unhealthy? What has happened in their life?*

Look at photos of people or strangers in the street for ideas.

3 *Now imagine being that person. Blindfold yourself and sit in a quiet room to help you focus.*

WHAT NEXT? *Imagine what your character would do if certain things happened. For example, what if they dropped a full bag of shopping...*

saw a lost dog...

... or had a call from an old friend?

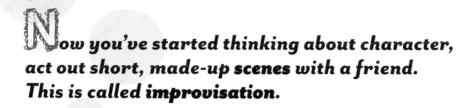

Just imagine...

Now you've started thinking about character, act out short, made-up **scenes** with a friend. This is called **improvisation**.

1 *Decide who you're going to be and where the scene takes place. How about two friends at a bus stop?*

2 *Work out a few details to set the scene. Perhaps it's after school, getting dark, and starting to rain.*

3 *Think of a problem to get the characters talking. What if the bus is late, or one of you spots something unusual in the other's bag, or you think you're being spied on?*

4 *Decide how long your scene will be—say two minutes—and set a timer. Start acting and see what happens!*

Don't try to include too much action.

WHAT NEXT? *Try a range of improvisations. Go to page 23 for some ideas to get you started.*

Show time!

Performing in a play is fun, but it takes practice. You need to learn your **lines**, remember **stage directions**, and get into character.

Reading scripts

Start by reading the whole **script**. Make sure you understand it. Highlight or copy out your lines and memorize them. Ask a friend to test you!

 Look at other people's lines, too, so you know when to say yours.

Keep your script with you at first to check if you forget a line.

Make it real

Think about your character. This will help you work out how to say your lines. For example, a script could include these lines:

Jack: *Where are you going?*
Lily: *I just need some fresh air.*

Depending on who Jack and Lily are, these lines could be spoken in many different ways!

WHAT NEXT? *Make a note of where to stand on stage and any moves you need to make. The **director** of the play may tell you what to do.*

13

Cool costumes

Acting is the perfect excuse to dress up! A good costume helps you get into character and makes a play really entertaining.

Keep it simple

You don't always need a fancy costume —keep it simple and let the audience use their imagination. Search in thrift stores for useful clothes, or reuse old Halloween costumes.

Hats, wigs, and scarves are often cheap and easy to buy.

Sheets, curtains, and other large pieces of fabric are useful. They can be cloaks for soldiers...

Fasten with a brooch or big safety pin.

Make sure your costume fits well and doesn't get in the way when you move.

... shawls for beggars...

Cut the fabric roughly and sew on patches.

... or tunics for kings, queens, or even aliens!

Add a belt and sew on extra decoration.

WHAT NEXT? *Try making masks to wear when performing. They look very dramatic on stage—but make sure your voice isn't muffled.*

Amazing makeup

Stage makeup helps the audience see your face clearly, and it helps to identify your character—especially if you're playing a strange creature or a scary villain!

Makeup effects

1 To look old, scrunch up your face to see where lines and wrinkles form.

2 Go over these lines with dark **face paint** on a thin brush. Smudge them a little so they don't look like stripes.

1 For a vampire face, dab white face paint all over your face using a sponge or brush. Avoid your eyes and mouth.

Test face paints on a small patch of skin first to check you aren't **allergic** to them.

2 Use rusty red or black to highlight the shadows on your face.

eye sockets

temples

sides of nose

under cheekbones

3 Use a thin brush to add details such as black lips, bushy eyebrows, and a **widow's peak** on your hairline.

WHAT NEXT? Make fake blood: mix two tablespoons of corn syrup, a few drops of red and yellow food coloring, and a tablespoon of instant coffee dissolved in a little hot water. Dab it on bandages.

Perfect props

Good props help to set the scene and make characters interesting. You only need a few, so choose them well— don't clutter the stage!

Think big

The audience won't be able to see tiny props, so pick a few big items. If your play is set in a living room, have just an armchair and table —don't add ornaments and other small items.

Try using crates or boxes as chairs or tables, or stand on them so the audience can see and hear you well.

Effects props

It's fun to use props offstage to make great sound effects!

Tap together the heels then the toes of a pair of shoes for footsteps.

Open and close umbrellas to make the noise of flapping wings.

👍 *Try recording sound effects, then play them loudly during the performance.*

Crumple potato chip packets or cellophane for a crackling fire.

Snap a carrot to sound like a bone breaking, or rip apart crisp lettuce for a sickening bone crunch.

WHAT NEXT?
*Why not make your props with **papier-mâché** or cardboard? You can also paint on fabric or big sheets of paper to create a **backdrop**.*

Fake fights

Action-packed plays often include fake fights. They need planning, teamwork, and practice. Have fun and remember: no one should really get hurt!

Hair pull

The secret of this clever routine is that the "victim" does all the work.

1 The attacker puts a clenched fist on top of the victim's head, as if grabbing a handful of hair.

attacker

victim

2 The victim grabs the fist with both hands and pretends to be pulled around. In fact they hold the fist in place.

👍 This works best if the victim acts being in pain!

Take that!

Practice this "slap" in slow motion first.

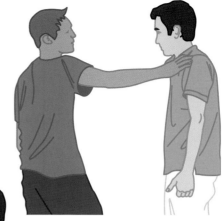

1 The attacker puts the non-hitting hand on the victim's shoulder to check they are the right distance apart.

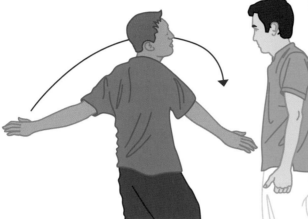

2 He swings the other arm back to prepare to slap.

The non-hitting arm moves down.

WHAT NEXT?

Try falling over after being "hit". Bend your legs, sit down, and roll backwards. Land on one side so you don't hurt your back.

3 The arm swings up, but slaps the attacker's other hand rather than the victim. The victim jerks when the slap sounds, as if hit.

Glossary

allergic
Very sensitive to something, which makes your body react badly, for example, making you feel itchy or giving you a rash.

backdrop
A painted cloth or other covering that hangs down at the back of the stage.

director
The person in charge of putting on a play. They decide how the play should be presented, and arrange stage directions, costumes, props, and scenery.

face paint
Paint designed to be used on skin and wash off easily. Never use ordinary paints on your face, as the ingredients could make it sore or itchy.

gestures
Body movements, especially of the hands and head.

improvisation
Acting done with little or no planning beforehand, making it up as you go along.

lines
The words a character speaks in a play.

papier-mâché
Layers of paper mixed with paste and molded to create models, which harden when dry.

scene
A piece of acting or section of a play.

script
A printed copy of all the spoken words in a play, as well as any stage directions.

stage directions tell actors where to stand and how to speak, or list lighting and sound effects.
Instructions in a script or given by the director. They may

widow's peak
A V-shaped point of hair in the middle of the forehead.

Improvisation ideas

Here are some ideas for improvisation scenes.
Each involves two people but you could include more.
Pick one and plan it for a few minutes, then act it out.

✿ *A child tells their mother about a problem at school.*
✿ *A reporter interviews a lottery winner.*
✿ *Two friends hear a thump on the roof while babysitting.*
✿ *A customer in a restaurant complains to the waiter.*
✿ *Two people who hate each other are stuck in an elevator.*
✿ *A father sees his son getting out of a police car.*

Web sites

www.acting-school-stop.com
Find lots of online acting lessons, videos, and advice.

www.snazaroo.com/beginners-guide
Discover fun face-painting techniques and ideas.

www.epicsound.com/sfx
Look at all kinds of weird and wonderful ways of making sound effects!

Index